OUR HEAVENLY FATHER

OUR HEAVENLY FATHER

Faith and Life Series

BOOK ONE

Ignatius Press, San Francisco
Catholics United for the Faith, New Rochelle

Nihil Obstat: Rev. Msgr. Daniel V. Flynn. J.C.D.
               Censor Librorum
Imprimatur: + Joseph T. O'Keefe, D.D.
               Vicar General, New York

Director: Rev. Msgr. Eugene Kevane, Ph.D.
Assistant Director and General Editor: Barbara M. Nacelewicz
Writer: Daria Sockey

Catholics United for the Faith, Inc., and Ignatius Press gratefully acknowledge the guidance and assistance of Reverend Monsignor Eugene Kevane, former Director of the Pontifical Catechetical Institute, Diocese of Arlington, Virginia, in the production of this series. The series intends to implement the authentic approach in Catholic catechesis given to the Church in the recent documents of the Holy See and in particular the Conference of Joseph Cardinal Ratzinger on "Sources and Transmission of Faith".

Excerpts from *The Penny Catechism* (Prow Books, Kenosha, WI, 1970). Excerpts from the Pius X *Catechism of Christian Doctrine* (Center for Family Catechetics, 1980). Catholics United for the Faith and Ignatius Press are grateful for permissions to reprint copyrighted material.

Contents

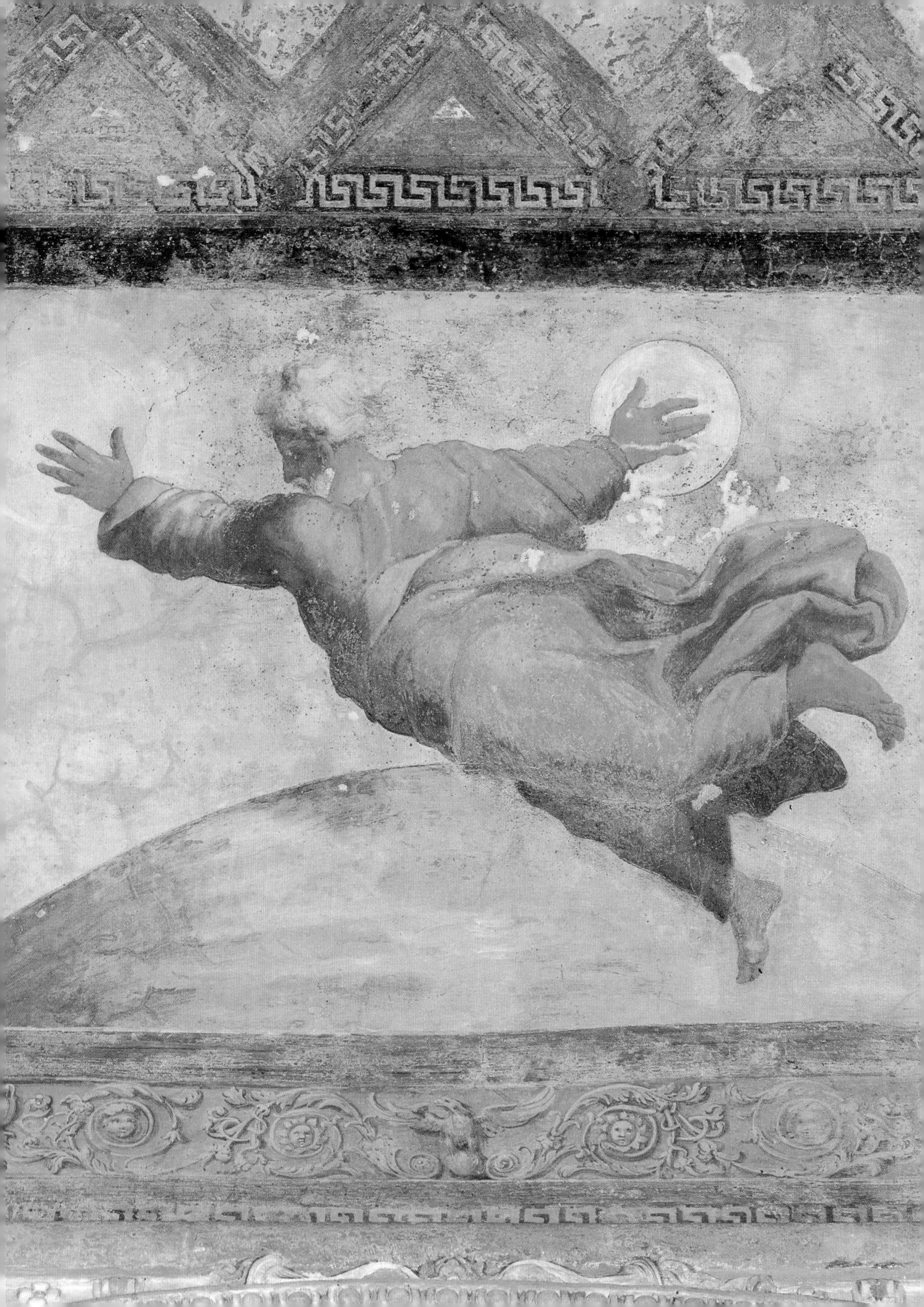

1   God Is Our Father

Did you know that you have a father who is not the man you call Dad? He is your father, your parents' father, and your grandparents' father. He is the father of all of us. He is God.

God is the one who made us. And God made the world we live in, too. God made flowers, vegetables, trees, and animals. God made the sun and the stars and the big, blue sky. He also made rivers and lakes and oceans, and everything there is.

Why did God make you? God made you because He wants you. And He wants you because He loves you very much. Because God loves you, He watches over you day and night. He does this by providing you with all the things you need. So the food we eat and the things we need to make clothes and houses all come from God.

God gives you your family and the people who take care of you and all the people you love. God made many things you like, things like warm sunshine and snow, and lots of water to swim in. And He didn't forget to make all the animals that make us happy.

How good your Father is! We should give thanks to God for all these gifts, like this:

Thank you, God, for everything!

When you talk to God, He always hears what you say. That is what praying is—just talking to God.

God wants you to call Him Father. So we can remember, He even gave us a prayer that begins that way:

"Our Father, Who art in Heaven. . . ."

We Pray:

OUR FATHER

Our Father, Who art in Heaven, hallowed be Thy Name; Thy Kingdom come; Thy will be done on earth as it is in Heaven. Give us this day our daily bread, and forgive us our trespasses, as we forgive those who trespass against us; and lead us not into temptation, but deliver us from evil. *Amen.*

Words to Know:

Our Father

2   Heaven Is Our Home

The last lesson had the prayer called the "Our Father". It began, "Our Father, Who art in Heaven". You know who "Our Father" is, don't you? In this prayer, the word "art" means "are".

And do you know what Heaven is? Heaven is God's home, and Heaven is the most wonderful place there is.

Now close your eyes and think of the most beautiful place you have ever seen. Think of the best time you ever had. Think of the things you love to do and the things that taste best. Well, Heaven is better than all of that!

Now comes the best part: God wants you to come to live with Him in Heaven someday. In Heaven you will be happy with God for ever and ever. And in Heaven no one is ever sad or hurt or crying. You can pray:

Thank You, God, my Father, for wanting to share Your home with me.

Words to Know:

Heaven

We Pray:

THE SIGN OF THE CROSS

When we talk to our Father in Heaven, we often begin:

In the Name of the Father, and of the Son, and of the Holy Spirit. *Amen.*

While we say the words, we make a big cross by touching with the right hand first the forehead, then the chest, the left shoulder, and finally the right shoulder.

3   God Watches Over Everything

God is everywhere, not just in Heaven. You cannot see God, but He looks after you all the time, wherever you are.

God is all powerful, which means that He can do anything. And no one is stronger than God.

And God knows *everything*. He knows what every fish and bug and bird is doing right now. He knows what you are doing and even what you are thinking.

God created all things—every single thing. "Create" means to make something out of nothing. Once there was only God: there was no light, no outer space, no earth, no water, nothing but God. Then God said, "Let there be light! Let there be sky! Let there be land and water!" And there it was, just like that, just the way God said.

God created angels too. Angels are like God in one way because they do not have bodies. They are invisible.

All the angels were very good when God created them. Then some of the angels turned away from God. That means they became bad; they became devils. But the good angels stayed with God to be His helpers.

Because God is all good, everything about Him is good. He takes care of all that He has made, like the stars and the planets, the animals, and the trees, and everything. But, above all, God cares for you.

Q. 1 *Who created us?*
God created us.

Q. 2 *Where is God?*
God is in Heaven, on earth, and in every place.

Q. 3 *Does God know all things?*
Yes, God knows all things, even our thoughts.

Q. 4 *Can God do all things?*
God can do all that He wills to do.

Q. 5 *Why is God called "the Creator of Heaven and earth"?*
God is called the Creator of Heaven and earth because He made them out of nothing.

Q. 6 *What are angels?*
Angels are invisible ministers of God, and they are also our guardians.

Words to Know:

create   angels   devils

4   God's Special Gifts

Once upon a time, not long ago, there was *no you*! Then God decided He wanted a girl or a boy like you very much. So He made you. He made you come to life, so very tiny, inside your mother's body. Then, when the right time came, you were born.

God gave you a body that can do all sorts of things. Your body can run and it can climb and jump and play. And God gave you eyes that are looking at this book right now, and ears that can listen to a story, or music, or any sound. And you can taste ice cream with your tongue, and touch puppies with your fingers, and smell cookies with your nose. God gave you all these wonderful things.

God also gave you a soul, a *very* important thing. The soul is the part of you that can think, and love, and choose what to do. Because you have a soul you can laugh at something funny. You can understand a story, too, and you can tell what is right and what is wrong—all because you have a soul. And your soul is the part of you that will never die.

Your body and your soul are very special to God. They are so special that He gave you a guardian angel to help you take care of them. Your angel is always looking after you because he is your very own angel. Your guardian angel helps you to do what is right because he is your friend.

Here is a prayer you can say:

Thank you, dear Father, for the wonderful gifts You have given me. *Amen.*

Words to Know:

body   soul   guardian angel

We Pray:

PRAYER TO MY GUARDIAN ANGEL

Angel of God, my guardian dear,
To whom God's love commits me here,
Ever this day be at my side,
To light and guard, to rule and guide. *Amen.*

21

5   Adam and Eve

Long, long ago, God made the world. Then He made the first man and the first woman, and they were called Adam and Eve.

God gave them a beautiful place to live in. It was called the Garden of Eden. In this garden there were trees with lots of good things to eat on them. Adam and Eve had every single thing they wanted. They were never sick, they were never hurt, and they never had to die. All the animals were their friends, too.

God had given Adam and Eve a very special gift: He shared with them His very own kind of life. That means that, with God's life in their souls, Adam and Eve could live for ever.

God gives this gift to us, too. The life of God in our souls is called grace. Because there is grace in our souls, we are able to go to Heaven. And because we have the gift of grace, we are God's children.

We call Adam and Eve our first parents because all the people of the world came from them.

Q. 7 *Who were the first man and woman?*
The first man and woman were Adam and Eve.

Words to Know:

Adam   Eve   grace

26

6   A Sad Story

One day, God gave Adam and Eve a test. He told them never to eat the fruit from one of the trees in the garden. Adam and Eve were good and obeyed God for a while.

But one day, the devil pretended he was a snake and came into the garden. He told Eve to go ahead and try some of the forbidden fruit from the tree. He said it would make her just as smart as God.

Eve knew that she should obey God, but she listened to the devil instead, and she ate the fruit. Then she gave some to Adam and he ate it too. This was the very first sin. Sin is saying, "No" to God. And that is what Adam and Eve did.

So Adam and Eve had to leave the lovely garden. Now they had to work for their food. And now they had to die some day. Worst of all, Adam and Eve lost the gift of grace. Without God's life in their souls, Adam and Eve could not go to Heaven. Adam and Eve were very sad and very sorry.

Adam and Eve lost God's gift of grace for all of us too. Now everyone is born with the sin of Adam and Eve. It is called *original sin*.

God felt sorry for Adam and Eve because He still loved them. He felt sorry for all the people who would come after them too. So He made them a promise. He promised to send a Savior. The Savior would win back God's grace and open the gates of Heaven for us again.

Q. 8 *What is sin?*
Sin is an offense against God, by any thought, word, deed, or omission against the law of God.

Q. 9 *What is original sin?*
Original sin is that guilt and stain of sin which we inherit from Adam, who was the origin and head of all mankind.

Words to Know:

sin   original sin   promise   Savior

"*I will look with favor on the faithful in the land, that they may dwell with me . . .*"

(*Psalm 101:6*)

7　　A Time of Waiting

God promised to send a Savior. But the Savior did not come right away. The people had to wait for years and years. While they waited, some of them learned to love and obey God.

Noah was one of these people. Although many others did not want to obey God, Noah always did what God asked. That is why God decided to wash the earth clean with a flood and begin again with Noah and his family.

So He told Noah to build an ark, which is a big boat. Then God told Noah to fill the ark with all the different kinds of animals. After all the animals were in the boat, God told Noah and his family to climb inside and close the door very tight. Once they were inside, it started raining very hard. Soon there was a flood. But because Noah and his family obeyed God, they were safe and dry and cozy inside the ark when the great flood came.

Later on, there was another man who loved and served God, and his name was Abraham. He always did what God wanted, even when it was hard. God promised to make Abraham the beginning of a great nation. And from these people the Savior would be born. Some of Abraham's descendants are still among us today. They are the people we call the Jews.

Words to Know:

Noah Abraham ark

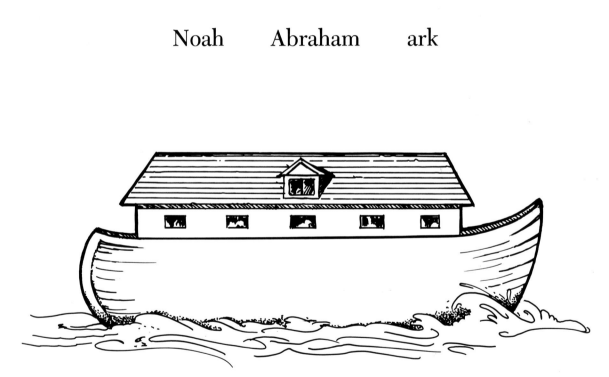

8   Getting Ready For the Savior

Many more years passed. The descendants of Abraham were still waiting for the Savior. God did not forget: He kept sending holy men called prophets to get everyone ready for the Savior.

Moses was the first prophet. Moses was very important because God gave him the Ten Commandments.

The Ten Commandments are God's laws for every one of us. These laws help us to know how God wants us to live. When people obeyed God's laws, they were getting ready for the coming of the Savior.

"I put the Law You have given before all the gold and silver in the world."

(Psalm 119:72)

Then, when it was almost time for the Savior to come, God sent the last prophet. He was Saint John the Baptist. Saint John was Jesus' cousin. He lived and prayed in the desert, and he told people to be sorry for their sins. He also told them that the Savior would come very soon.

Words to Know:

John the Baptist   prophets   Moses
Ten Commandments

Q. 10 *What are the Commandments of God?*
The Commandments of God are the moral laws which God gave to Moses on Mount Sinai.

9   Mary Hears Some Wonderful News

Finally, the time came for the Savior to come into the world. There was one last thing to get ready.

There was a girl named Mary. Mary lived in a town called Nazareth, and God loved her so much that He gave her the gift of grace that Adam had lost for everyone else. Mary was free from original sin from the very first moment of her life. She loved God so much that in her whole life she never committed even one single sin. Everything she did made God happy.

Now when Mary grew up, God sent the angel Gabriel to visit her. Gabriel told Mary some wonderful news. He said that God wanted her to be the Mother of His Son, the promised Savior.

Mary trusted that God knew what was best. So Mary said, "I am God's servant. Let it be done to me as you say." That is how Mary became the Mother of Jesus.

God's very own Son came down from Heaven to live with us. God also chose a special man named Joseph to be Mary's husband and to take care of Jesus. Since God is Jesus' real father, we call Joseph the foster-father of Jesus.

Words to Know:

Jesus   Mary   Joseph   Gabriel   Nazareth

Q. 11 *From whom was Jesus Christ born?*
Jesus Christ was born of Mary ever-virgin.

Q. 12 *Was anyone ever preserved from original sin?*
Mary alone has been preserved from original sin.

10   The Savior Is Born

One day, Mary and Joseph had to travel to Bethlehem. They looked and looked for a place to stay, but every inn was full and no one took them in. So they had to stay in a stable, a place where animals were kept.

That is where Jesus was born. Mary laid him in a manger because there was no cradle for him. The Son of God, our Savior, came here to earth as a poor, tiny, helpless baby.

Angels from Heaven appeared in the sky. They sang, "Glory to God in the highest. Peace on earth to men of good will."

Some shepherds saw the angels and they were afraid. "Do not be afraid", said the angels. "We have good news for you and for all people. Today in Bethlehem a Savior has been born! You will find him lying in a manger." Then the angels left.

The shepherds were amazed. They said, "Let us go to Bethlehem and see this Child that the angels have told us about."

The shepherds hurried away and found Jesus, Mary, and Joseph. They knelt down and worshipped their Savior. And they remembered to thank God the Father for sending us His Son.

Christmas is the birthday of Jesus. And it is important because if Jesus had not come, we could not go to Heaven, ever. There would be no Christmas trees, no presents, no Christmas lights, no Christmas songs, nothing to make you happy.

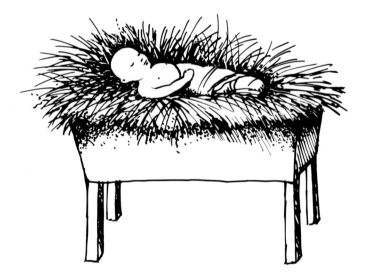

But Jesus *did* come. And so we have a wonderful time every year to celebrate His birthday. We can pray:

Thank you, dear Jesus, for coming down from Heaven to save us. Thank you for Christmas time. Help us to get ready for your coming this year. *Amen.*

Words to Know:

Bethlehem   manger   shepherds   Christmas

Q. 13 *Where was Jesus Christ born?*
Jesus Christ was born at Bethlehem, in a stable, and was placed in a manger.

Q. 14 *Who is Jesus Christ?*
Jesus Christ is the second Person of the Holy Trinity, the Son of God made man.

Q. 15 *Why did the Son of God become man?*
The Son of God became man to save us from sin and to regain Heaven for us.

ET APERTIS THESAVRIS SVIS OBTVLERVT EI AVRVM THVS 7 MIRRAM .MACEI. I . C.

44

11 Three Wise Men Arrive

Jesus came to save everybody. He loves the people of every part of the world and He loves them very, very much.

Three wise men came to Bethlehem from a faraway land. They did not get lost because they followed a star that brought them to Jesus. The wise men knew that Jesus was a great king—the greatest king of all! So they knelt before Jesus and gave Him gifts fit for a king.

Jesus was glad to see the wise men. Although He was a baby, He really was their God and King.

Can you do what the wise men did? Can you visit Jesus and give Him gifts? Yes, you can! Jesus is always waiting for you in Church. You can visit Him any time the Church is open.

If you are at home, you can visit Jesus, too. All you have to do is stop what you are doing and talk to Him. God is everywhere and can always hear you.

Your gift to Jesus is your love for Him. Your prayers are a gift to Him. Your good deeds are a gift to Him. Each time you choose right over wrong, it is a gift to Jesus.

Words to Know:

wise men   king

"Where is He who has been born King of the Jews? For we have seen His star in the east, and have come to worship Him."

(Matthew 2:2)

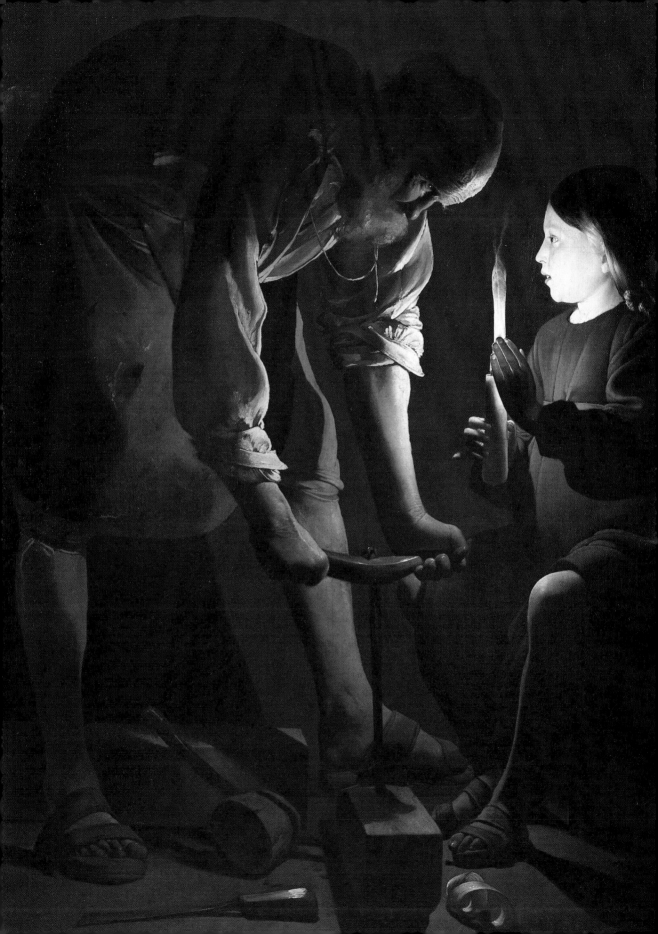

12   Jesus Grows Up

The boy Jesus lived and worked and played in a little house in Nazareth. Jesus is the Son of God. Mary is His mother. And Saint Joseph is His foster-father.

Saint Joseph did everything for Jesus just like a real father should. Saint Joseph was a carpenter and made things with wood. Jesus liked to help him in the shop because He wanted to learn to be a carpenter, like Joseph.

Jesus loved His parents. He obeyed them and helped them with their work and He grew up and was strong and good. Jesus did all these things to show us how to love our families. When we love and obey, it makes our Heavenly Father happy with us.

Saint Joseph . . .

Foster-father of the Son of God . . .

Head of the Holy Family . . .

Joseph most just . . .

Joseph most strong . . .

Joseph most obedient . . .

Joseph most faithful . . .

Pillar of families . . .

Protector of Holy Church . . .

Pray for us.

Q. 16 *Wasn't Saint Joseph the father of Jesus Christ?*
Saint Joseph was believed to be His true father, although actually he was not.

Words to Know:

carpenter   obey

52

13 Jesus Begins His Work

When Jesus had grown up and was thirty years old, He left Nazareth. He knew it was time to begin His work. Jesus walked from town to town and taught. He was a teacher, and he wanted everyone to learn about God.

He told people things about God that they never knew before, and He taught them how to love God better. Sometimes Jesus would teach big crowds, lots and lots of people. And sometimes He spoke to them one at a time.

Jesus liked to spend time with children. He liked to tell them how much their Heavenly Father loved them. He put His arms around the children and then He gave them His blessing.

Jesus picked twelve men to be His helpers. They are called the Apostles. The Apostles left their homes and went everywhere with Jesus. They listened to His teachings and then they told other people about Jesus.

We, too, can be Apostles and follow Jesus if we listen to what our teacher and parents say about Him, and tell others what we have learned, and remember that Jesus is always near us.

Words to Know:

teacher   Apostles

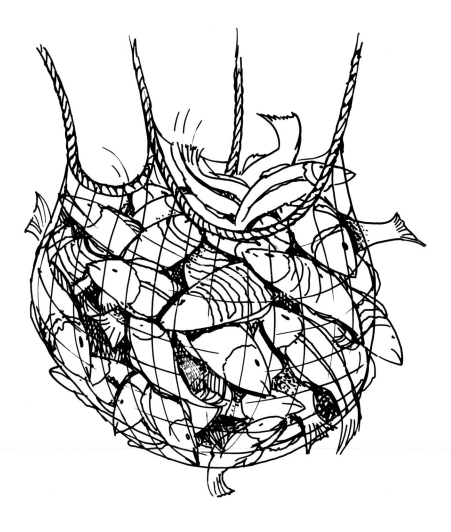

"Follow me and I will make you become fishers of men."

(Mark 1:17)

14   Jesus Tells The Good News

Jesus and the twelve Apostles went from town to town. Jesus told everyone the Good News everywhere He went.

The Good News was about God's love for all. Jesus told them that God is their Father Who loves them very much. And He told them that God wants them to be His children. He also said that God wants them to live in the Kingdom of Heaven.

Many people were happy to hear this Good News because they had waited all their lives for Jesus to come and show them the way to Heaven. Jesus taught them many other things, like how to pray, how to love God, and how to love one another. He came to show us all the way to Heaven.

We can hear the Good News of Jesus, too. The friends of Jesus wrote down the things He said and did while He was living here on earth. You can read about them in a book called the Bible.

The Bible has other things in it, too. It tells the story of Adam and Eve's sin and Noah and Abraham. It also has prayers and songs.

Words to Know:

Good News   Bible

15   Jesus Does Wonderful Things

To show us that He was really the Son of God, Jesus did many wonderful things that were beyond human power. We call these things miracles. Here are some of Jesus' miracles:

One time, Jesus finished teaching five thousand people. Then it was late and everyone was hungry, but there wasn't enough food for everyone. So Jesus took five loaves of bread and two fishes and made them into enough food for all of them, all five thousand hungry people.

Another day Jesus and the Apostles were out on a boat when a big storm came. The Apostles were afraid the boat would sink so they called to Jesus, "Save us, Lord." Jesus told the wind and waves to be quiet, and everything grew calm, just like that! Only God can make the weather obey.

Another time a man came to Jesus. "Please come to my house", he said. "My little girl is sick." Jesus was sad about this so He went with him. On the way, someone from the man's house met them and he said, "It is too late. She's dead." But Jesus went right on to the house and He took the child's hand. "Get up, little girl", said Jesus. The little girl opened her eyes and got up. Jesus had brought her back to life.

Jesus did many other miracles too. He made blind people see, He made deaf people hear, and He made sick people well.

Because Jesus is God, He could help anyone who asked Him for help. But He would only help them if it really was good for them, if it was for the best. Jesus wants you to ask Him for help when you need it, too. In the prayer Jesus gave us, we say, "Give us this day our daily bread", and that means asking for just about anything we need.

One day, some people carried a very sick man to Jesus. The man couldn't walk or even move his arms.

But before Jesus made him better, He said, "Your sins are forgiven." Then He said, "Get up and walk." The man got up and walked. He felt so much better because his sins were gone, too.

Because Jesus is God, He could heal the sick. Because Jesus is God, He can forgive sins. If we are sorry for our sins, Jesus will forgive them, too.

Words to Know:

miracle   forgive

64

16   We Believe in Jesus

Jesus is God's Son and the Savior of the world. He wants everyone to believe this because it is true. That is why He did all those miracles. And that is why He taught people. If you believe in Jesus, He will give you a reward, like in this real story:

Once there was a blind man. When Jesus was walking by, the blind man called out, "Jesus, help me." "What do you want me to do?" Jesus asked. "Please make me see", begged the blind man. "Because you believe that I can do this, you will see", Jesus said. And He cured the blind man then and there.

Another day, a man came to ask Jesus to cure his dying servant, who was at home. "Lord," the man said, "I am not worthy [that means 'not good enough'] for you to enter my house. But I know that if you just say one word, you can cure my servant from here." Jesus was so pleased with the man's faith that when the man came home, the servant was better. Jesus had cured him.

Jesus wants you to believe in Him too. You can pray:

Lord, I believe in You. Please help those who do not believe in You. *Amen.*

Words to Know:

believe

They did this:	And this is what happened:
The blind man believed in Jesus.	Jesus made him see.
The man with the dying servant believed in Jesus.	Jesus cured the servant.

You do this:	And this is what will happen:
You believe in Jesus.	Jesus will bring you to Heaven to be happy with Him for ever.

17   The Best Gift of All

Jesus knew He was going to die soon. He loved us so very much that He found a way to be with us after He died.

The special supper Jesus shared with His Apostles before He died is called the Last Supper. At the Last Supper, Jesus took bread and blessed it. He said, "Take this and eat it. *This is My Body.*" Then Jesus took a cup of wine and said, *"This is the cup of My Blood."* Jesus changed bread and wine into His own Body and Blood. When the Apostles ate this Bread, Jesus lived inside them.

Then Jesus gave His Apostles the power to change bread and wine into His Body and Blood. And the Apostles passed on this power to all the bishops and priests who came after them, right up to today.

The priest at your church has received this power. Because he has this power, when your priest offers Mass, he does what Jesus did at the Last Supper. When your priest says the words of Jesus, the bread and wine become the Body and Blood of Jesus. And when the people receive Holy Communion, Jesus comes to live in them. This is the best gift Jesus could have given us.

Words to Know:

Last Supper   Mass   priest
Holy Communion

"Jesus answered:
'I am the Bread of Life.
He who comes to Me will never be hungry;
he who believes in Me will never thirst. . . .
I am the living Bread
which has come down from Heaven.
Anyone who eats this Bread will live for ever
and the Bread that I shall give
is My flesh, for the life of the world.' "

(John 6:35, 51)

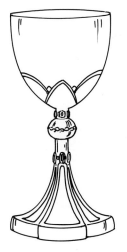

18   Jesus Dies for Us

The Last Supper happened on a Thursday. That night, after the Supper was over, Jesus went out to a garden to pray. He knew that soon He would be killed, but He wanted to give His life to save us. When soldiers came and took Jesus away the Apostles were afraid, but Jesus was brave. The next day, on Friday, they beat Him with whips. And they pressed a crown of thorns onto His head and made fun of Him.

Because Jesus was God He could have stopped them from hurting Him. But He didn't. That is because He wanted to suffer for us, because He loved us.

Later that day, bad men decided to kill Jesus. Jesus had to carry a heavy Cross through the city of Jerusalem and sometimes it made Him fall.

Mary met her Son on the way and she suffered very much when she saw the way people were hurting Jesus. Then a man named Simon helped Jesus to carry the Cross until they came to the top of a hill. That is where the soldiers nailed Jesus to the Cross. Mary and Saint John stood by Jesus the whole time.

After three hours, Jesus died. His friends took Him down from the Cross and buried Him.

Jesus died to make up for Adam's sin and for our sins, too. Jesus died to win back the gift of grace for us. Jesus died so that we could live in Heaven for ever and ever. We call the day He died Good Friday because it is good that Jesus died and opened up the gates of Heaven. You can pray:

Thank you, Jesus, for loving me so much. I am sorry my sins made You suffer. Thank You for giving Your life for me. *Amen.*

Words to Know:

Good Friday

Q. 17 *What were the chief sufferings of Christ?*
The chief sufferings of Christ were: *first*, His agony, and His sweat of blood in the Garden; *secondly*, His being scourged at the pillar, and crowned with thorns; and *thirdly*, His carrying His cross, His crucifixion, and His death between two thieves.

Q. 18 *Why did our Savior suffer?*
Our Savior suffered to atone for our sins, and to purchase for us eternal life.

19   Jesus Was Raised To New Life

On the third day after Jesus died, something wonderful happened. Jesus rose from the dead, which means that He came back to life! That day was the very first Easter Sunday. When He rose from the dead, Jesus worked His greatest miracle. We call it the Resurrection.

Mary and the Apostles were so happy to see Jesus alive again. And we are glad that our Savior is alive again, too.

At Mass on Easter Sunday we sing joyful songs that say:

"The Lord is risen!"
"Alleluia! Alleluia! Alleluia!"

Jesus won the gift of grace for us so now we, too, can come back to life after we die. We will go to Heaven to be with Jesus.

Words to Know:

Easter   Alleluia   Resurrection

Q. 19 *After His death, what did Jesus Christ do?*
After His death, Jesus Christ rose again from the dead, taking up His body which had been buried.

Q. 20 *How long did the body of Jesus Christ remain buried?*
The body of Jesus Christ remained buried from Friday evening to the day that we now call Easter Sunday

20 Jesus Begins the Church

Jesus was alive and with His Apostles again. But He was not going to stay on earth for ever. Then how could Jesus teach the people who would be born after He had gone back to Heaven? He did it by starting His Church.

People who belong to the Church can learn about Jesus and receive the gift of grace, just as if Jesus were still on earth.

Jesus made His Apostles the leaders of His Church and they were the first bishops. Then He made Peter the head of the Apostles and Peter was the very first Pope.

Do you know who our Pope is today? Do you know who your bishop is?

Words to Know:

Catholic Church   Pope   bishop   Peter

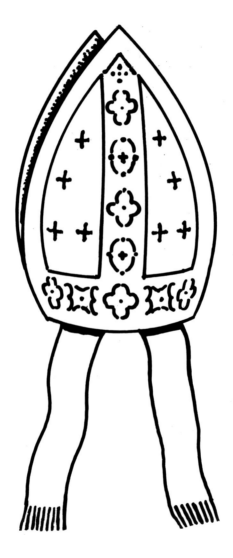

Q. 21 *What is the Church?*
The Church is the society of true Christians, that is, baptized persons who profess the Faith and teaching of Jesus Christ.

Q. 22 *By whom was the Church founded?*
The Church was founded by Jesus Christ.

Q. 23 *Who are the legitimate pastors of the Church?*
The true pastors of the Church are the Pope and the bishops united with him.

Q. 24 *Who is the Pope?*
The Pope is the successor of Saint Peter. He is the visible head of the entire Church.

21 Jesus Goes Back to Heaven

Jesus spent forty days with His Apostles after He rose from the dead. He told them many things that they should know. Then it was time for Him to leave. It was time for Him to go back to God, His Father.

So He took the Apostles to the top of a mountain. "Go", He said. "Teach everyone and baptize them in the name of the Father and of the Son and of the Holy Spirit." Jesus promised to be with them always even if they could not see Him. And He promised to send the Holy Spirit to help them, too. Then Jesus rose up into the sky. We call this the Ascension.

The Apostles watched and watched until they could not see Jesus any more. Then two angels came. They said, "Someday, Jesus will come again." Jesus will come again at the end of the world.

" . . . as they were looking on, He was lifted up, and a cloud took Him out of their sight."

(Acts 1:9)

Q. 25 *What did Jesus Christ do after His Resurrection?*
After His Resurrection, Jesus Christ remained on earth forty days. Then He ascended to Heaven.

Words to Know:

Ascension   Holy Spirit

22 The Holy Spirit Comes

For nine days, the Apostles waited for the Holy Spirit to come to them. They stayed in a house with Mary and prayed and prayed. On the tenth day something wonderful happened. The Apostles heard the sound of a great wind. And then the Holy Spirit came!

The Holy Spirit filled their souls with grace and He filled their hearts with love for God. He helped them to remember and to understand all the things Jesus had taught them. He made them very brave.

Now the Apostles could go out and tell all the world about Jesus, just as He asked them to. So the Apostles went out. Peter began to teach the Good News. "Believe in Jesus, be baptized, and you will be saved", Peter said.

Many people believed Peter's words, and they were baptized that very day. Already the Church was starting to grow.

The Holy Spirit is alive in the Church today. He helps the Pope and the bishops to teach the truth about God. And He helps us to love one another and become holy.

> Holy Spirit, come to me
> And live here in my soul.
> Fill the heart You made for me
> With grace and make me whole.

Words to Know:

Holy Spirit   Baptism

SECVND
VM·MAT·
LIBER
GENERA
TIONIS

IESV
CHR
ISTI·
FILII·D
AVID·

INITIV
EVANGE
LII IESV
CHRIST

SECVN
DVM
LVCAM
FVIT·
IN·DIE

IN PRI
VNCIPIO·
VM·AT·VEP
IOAM·ET·
NNERBVM·

HERO
DIS·RE
GIS·

23   The Blessed Trinity

There is only one God. But there are three Persons in God: The Father, the Son, and the Holy Spirit. The Father is God. The Son is God. The Holy Spirit is God. But together They are one God.

We call the three Persons in one God the Blessed Trinity. God the Father is the first Person of the Blessed Trinity. God the Son is the second Person of the Blessed Trinity. He became the man Whom we call Jesus and Who died to save us from sin. God the Holy Spirit is the third Person of the Blessed Trinity. He helps us to pray and to love.

The three Persons of the Trinity had no beginning. They always were and always will be.

The three Persons are equal. The Father is not greater than the Son. The Son is not greater than the Spirit.

We know there are three Persons in one God because Jesus told us about it. But we cannot really understand how God can be both three and one. That is called a mystery and we will have to wait until Heaven to understand it better. But it can help if you think about a family. In a family there are the mother, father, and children, all different persons, but they are one family. In the Blessed Trinity there are three Persons, but one God.

We often begin our prayers by calling on the Blessed Trinity. We say, "In the name of the Father, and of the Son, and of the Holy Spirit." When we say these words, we make the Sign of the Cross on our bodies. And it reminds us that Jesus saved us by dying on a Cross.

When my soul is filled with grace, the Blessed Trinity lives in me!

Words to Know:

Trinity   mystery   God the Father
God the Son   God the Holy Spirit

Q. 26 *Who is the first Person of the Holy Trinity?*
The first Person of the Holy Trinity is the Father.

Q. 27 *Who is the second Person of the Holy Trinity?*
The second Person of the Holy Trinity is the Son.

Q. 28 *Who is the third Person of the Holy Trinity?*
The third Person of the Holy Trinity is the Holy Spirit.

Q. 29 *Has God always existed?*
God always has been and always will be.

We Pray:

GLORY BE

Glory be to the Father, and to the Son, and to the Holy Spirit, as it was in the beginning, is now, and ever shall be, world without end. *Amen.*

24 God Gives You His Life.

When Adam sinned, it meant that all the people born after him would be guilty, too. You were born with the guilt of original sin on your soul. That means that when you were born, there was no grace in your soul.

But Baptism washes away the guilt of original sin. When you are baptized, your soul is filled with the grace that Jesus won for you. That way you can get to Heaven.

Baptism makes you a child of God. And Baptism makes you a member of God's family, which is the Church.

Jesus said to His Apostles, "Go, and baptize all people." Like the Apostles, the priest is Jesus' helper. That is why the priest baptizes people.

When the priest baptizes a baby, he pours water on the baby's head and says, "I baptize you in the name of the Father, and of the Son, and of the Holy Spirit." Now the baby is a child of God. Now the baby's soul is holy and pleasing to God.

Ask your parents about your own baptism. They can tell you all about when you were baptized. Maybe they even took a picture of your baptism.

Q. 30 *How is original sin taken away?*
Original sin is taken away by Baptism.

Q. 31 *What is Baptism?*
Baptism is the sacrament which makes us Christians, that is, followers of Jesus Christ, sons of God, and members of the Church.

"Just as a human body, though it is made up of many parts, is a single unit because all these parts though many, make one body, so it is with Christ. In the one Spirit we were all baptized. . . ."

(1 Corinthians 12:12—13)

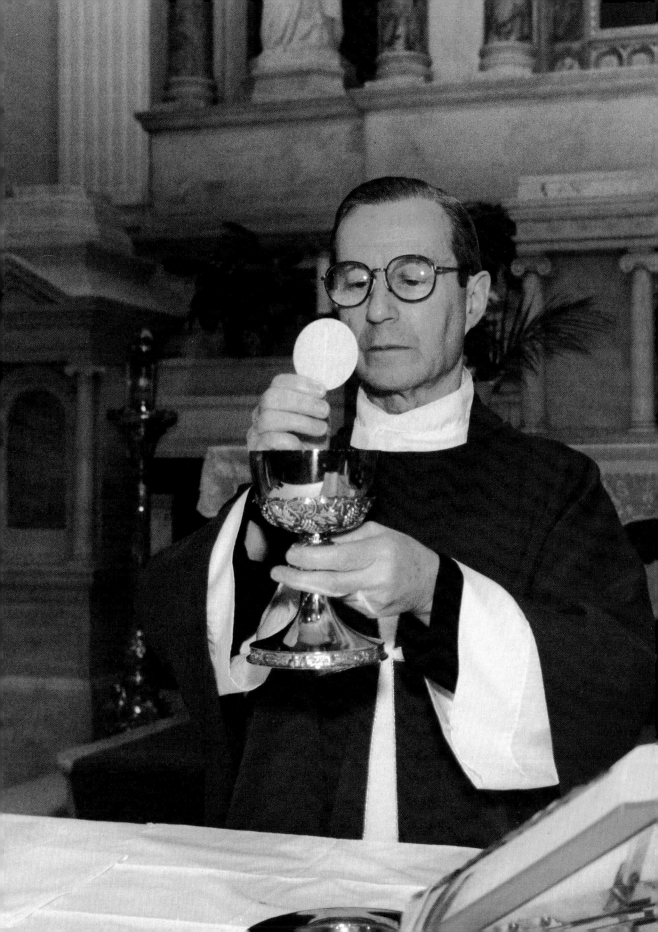

25 Many Gifts from God

God has given you many gifts. He made you. He gave you a wonderful world to live in. He gave you your family. God also sent His Son to be your Savior. And He gave you the gift of grace in the sacrament of Baptism.

Do you wonder how you can thank God for all He has given you? One of the best things you can do is to be quiet at Mass and to listen and to join in the prayers.

Because at every Mass we hear God's word, God is speaking to us. We listen to a special message from God's book, which is called the Holy Bible. And we hear the Good News about Jesus from a part of the Bible called the Gospel.

Jesus is with us at Mass. He offers Himself to God the Father at every Mass, just as He did on Good Friday. We can offer ourselves with Jesus, too.

At every Mass we should remember the Last Supper that Jesus had with the Apostles and how He changed the bread and wine into His Body and Blood. God has given priests the power to do what Jesus did. That is why the priest takes bread in his hands and says the words of Jesus:

"This is My Body"

and the bread becomes the Body of Jesus. Then the priest takes the cup of wine and says:

"This is the cup of My Blood"

and the wine becomes the Blood of Jesus.

We do not see Jesus on the altar, but He is really there. Jesus is God and He can do anything.

Someday, you will be able to receive Jesus in Holy Communion. Then you will be closer to Him than ever before. Here is a prayer you can say:

Jesus, please come to me soon. I want so much to receive You. *Amen.*

Q. 32 *What is the Mass?*
The Mass is the sacrifice of the Body and the Blood of Jesus Christ, which is offered on the altar by the priest to God, under the appearances of bread and wine, in memory of the sacrifice of the Cross and in renewal of the sacrifice of the Cross.

Q. 33 *Why has Christ given Himself to us in the Holy Eucharist?*
Christ has given Himself to us in the Holy Eucharist to be the life and food of our souls. "He that eats Me, the same also shall live by Me"; "He that eats this bread shall live for ever." *(John 6:58, 59)*

Words to Know:

Gospel

26   Our Mother, Mary

Before Jesus went back to His Heavenly Father, He left us one more special gift. He gave us His Mother for our very own! From her place in Heaven she watches over you with so much love.

You can pray to your Blessed Mother when you need help. She will pray to God for you. She will help you to get to Heaven.

Jesus is the King of Heaven. Mary is the Queen. Mary is the Queen of all the angels and all the saints.

Mary is a special friend of children. She has asked all boys and girls to pray and make sacrifices so that there will be peace in the world.

"Jesus said to the disciple, 'There is your Mother.' "

(John 19:27)

We Pray:

HAIL MARY

Hail Mary, full of grace! The Lord is with thee. Blessed art thou among women, and blessed is the fruit of thy womb, Jesus.

Holy Mary, Mother of God, pray for us sinners, now and at the hour of our death. *Amen.*

Words to Know:

Queen of Heaven   sacrifice

Holy Mary . . .
Holy Mother of God . . .
Mother of divine grace . . .
Mother of Our Savior . . .
Health of the sick . . .
Help of Christians . . .
Queen of angels . . .
Queen of prophets . . .
Queen of Apostles . . .
Queen of all saints . . .
Queen of peace . . .

Pray for us.

27   Following Jesus

When we play Follow the Leader, we walk behind someone else and we do whatever the person in front of us does. The "Leader" doesn't take us to any place special because it is only a game.

But Jesus is our leader on the road of life and that's not a game, it is real. By following Him, we can come to the Kingdom of Heaven. By doing whatever Jesus does, we learn how to live as God's children.

These are some of the things Jesus did that we should follow. Jesus always obeyed His Mother and foster-father. He told them the truth. He did the work they asked Him to do. He was kind to everyone. He shared with others. He forgave those who hurt Him. You can do these things, too.

Jesus also showed us how to pray. To pray means to talk to God. You can say the prayers you have learned or you can tell God what you are thinking about. God is interested in anything you have to say and anything you think, or even feel.

Every morning when you wake up, you should kneel down and make the Sign of the Cross. You should offer God everything you will do and say and think that day. At night, you kneel down beside your bed and thank God for the things He gave you all during that day.

You ask Him to bless all those you love and all the people everywhere. And you try to remember if you did anything wrong that day, and then you can tell God you are sorry. And then you ask Him to make you a better boy or girl tomorrow.

Remember: you can pray any time or anywhere, and about anything. You can ask God to help people who are sick or unhappy. You can ask God to make you a saint.

Jesus taught us to love God with all our hearts. You can show God that you love Him, too. One way is to work hard to learn about Him. You can try to be good even when it is very hard. And you can go to Mass and learn to say the prayers of the Mass. With Jesus, you can offer yourself to the Father at Mass.

God has given you so many gifts. Your gift to God is to live as His good child.

Words to Know:

prayer   saint

Q. 34 *What is prayer?*
Prayer is a lifting up of the soul to God to know Him better, to adore Him, to thank Him, to tell Him we are sorry, and to ask Him for what we need.

28 Jesus Will Come Again

Do you know why you are here on earth? You are here to learn to know God, to love God, and to serve God. If you learn how to do these things, you will be ready to live with God for ever and ever in Heaven.

We are on earth for only a short time, but Heaven never ends. Heaven is our true home, the place where we will always be happy with Jesus, with Mary, and with those we love.

Someday the world will end. And then Jesus will come again. He will take all the good people to Heaven with Him. The souls of all the people who have died will be joined to their bodies again.

Do you want to start on the road to Heaven? All you have to do is try your best to love God every day. Ready! Set! Go!

"And when I go and prepare a place for you, I will come again and take you to Myself that where I am you may be also."

(John 14:3)

Q. 35 *Why did God make you?*
God made me to know Him, to love Him, and to serve Him in this world, and to be happy with Him for ever in Heaven.

Words to Know:

serve

We Go to Mass

One of God's laws says, "You must keep the Lord's Day holy." Sunday is the Lord's Day, because Jesus rose from the dead on a Sunday. That is why every Sunday we go to Church to worship God at Mass.

When we come into Church, we use holy water to make the Sign of the Cross. Before we take our seats, we genuflect to honor Jesus in the tabernacle. And then before Mass begins, we kneel down and talk to God for a while.

The priest comes in while we sing a hymn. He begins Mass with the Sign of the Cross: "In the name of the Father, and of the Son, and of the Holy Spirit. *Amen.*"

Then the priest asks us to think about how we have disobeyed God. And we think, "Dear Jesus, I am sorry for my sins. I want to love You more and more."

And then we usually say: "Glory to God in the highest!" We use the same words the angels sang at Bethlehem to praise God for His goodness.

After that we sit down and hear two readings and a Psalm from the Bible. We should listen carefully and try to understand God's message to us.

Then we stand and listen while the priest reads from

the Gospel. The Gospel is the part of the Bible that tells us what Jesus said and did. Through the words of the Gospel, Jesus teaches us about our Heavenly Father. Then the priest talks to us to help us understand God's word.

After that we stand and say the Creed. The Creed is what we believe about God and His Church.

Now it is time for the Offertory. That is when we offer gifts of bread and wine, and we offer our money to help take care of our Church. We offer ourselves with Jesus to God the Father.

At the Last Supper, Jesus changed bread and wine into His own Body and Blood. At Mass, the priest takes the place of Jesus. He takes a special round piece of bread and says the words of Jesus,

"This is My Body."

The bread is not bread anymore. It is the real Body of Jesus.

Next the priest takes the cup filled with wine and says,

"This is the cup of My Blood."

Now the wine is the Blood of Jesus. We worship Jesus when the priest holds Him up and tell Him how happy we are that He is with us.

Then we stand and say the prayer Jesus gave us, the "Our Father". We may give the Sign of Peace to each other to show that we want to love one another, just as Jesus taught us.

The people go up to receive Jesus in Holy Communion. Someday you will make your first Communion.

After a last prayer, the priest says, "The Mass is ended. Go in peace." And we answer, "Thanks be to God."

After the priest leaves, we should kneel down to thank Jesus and say goodbye to Him.

Thank you, Jesus, for the gift of the Mass. Help me to love God and others this week. *Amen.*

Words to Know:

worship   genuflect   creed

Words to Know

Abraham: A man who lived before Jesus. He always did what God wanted, even when it was hard. He is known as the father of the Jewish people.

Adam and Eve: The first man and woman God made. We call them our first parents because everyone came from them.

Alleluia: A word that means, "Praise God." We say this at Eastertime to show how happy we are that Jesus rose from the dead.

angels: Spirits made by God. Angels are God's helpers.

Apostles: The twelve friends of Jesus who went out to tell others about Jesus after He went back to Heaven. They became the first bishops.

ark: The boat that God told Noah to build to save himself, his family, and the animals from the great flood.

Ascension: The return of Jesus to Heaven forty days after Easter.

Baptism: Baptism takes away original sin. It gives grace to our souls and makes us children of God.

believe: To believe is to accept that Jesus is telling us the truth about Himself and His Father. And we know that Jesus is telling us the truth because God cannot lie.

Bethlehem: The town where Jesus was born.

Bible: The holy book that God gave us. It tells us about God's special people and about the beginning of the Church.

bishop: A man who has received the power from the Apostles to carry on their work. He takes care of a large group of Catholics.

body: The part of you that you can see. The other part of you is your soul.

carpenter: Someone who makes chairs, tables, and many other things out of wood. Joseph and Jesus were both carpenters.

Catholic Church: The followers of Jesus. The Pope and the bishops are the leaders of the Church.

Christmas: The birthday of Jesus.

create: To create is to make something out of nothing. God is our Creator. That means He made us and all things out of nothing.

Creed: What we believe about God and His Church.

devils: Bad angels who turned away from God.

Easter: The Sunday Jesus rose from the dead.

forgive: To forgive is to pardon someone who has done something wrong. Only God can forgive sins.

Gabriel: The angel that God sent to Mary. He told her that she would be Jesus' Mother.

genuflect: To kneel down on your right knee and then get up again.

God the Father: God the Father is God, the first Person of the Blessed Trinity.

God the Holy Spirit: God the Holy Spirit is God, the third Person of the Blessed Trinity.

God the Son: God the Son is Jesus, the second Person of the Blessed Trinity.

Good Friday: The day Jesus died on the Cross for our sins.

Good News: The message Jesus came to tell us and all the things He did for us.

Gospel: The Good News of Jesus. In the Gospels, Jesus' friends wrote down many of the things He said and did while He was living here on earth.

grace: The life of God in our souls.

guardian angel: A special angel given to each of us by God to help us.

Heaven: The place where God wants us to come to be happy with Him for ever.

Holy Communion: The receiving of the Body and Blood of Jesus.

Holy Spirit: The Holy Spirit is God, the third Person of the Blessed Trinity.

Jesus: Jesus is God, the second Person of the Blessed Trinity.

John the Baptist: The cousin of Jesus. John was the last of the prophets. He prepared people for the coming of Jesus.

Joseph: The foster-father of Jesus and husband of Mary.

king: Someone who rules over a land. Jesus is King not only of the whole world but of Heaven too.

Last Supper: The holy supper that Jesus had with His Apostles the night before He died. At the Last Supper Jesus gave us His Body and Blood.

manger: A wooden box used to hold food for animals. Mary had to use a manger for Baby Jesus' bed.

Mary: The Mother of Jesus. Mary is our Mother too.

Mass: At Mass, Jesus offers Himself to the Father just as He did on Good Friday.

miracle: Something wonderful that is done by the power of God and that only God can do.

Moses: The first prophet. God gave Moses the Ten Commandments.

mystery: Something that only God can understand completely. The Blessed Trinity is a mystery.

Nazareth: The town where Jesus lived with Mary and Joseph.

Noah: The good man who built the ark to save his family and the animals from the great flood.

obey: To obey is to do what we are told. We should obey God's laws.

original sin: The very first sin committed by Adam and Eve.

Our Father: The special prayer which Jesus gave us. We say it to our Father in Heaven.

Peter: The very first Pope. Peter was one of the twelve Apostles chosen by Jesus.

Pope: The man who holds the place of Jesus as head of the Church until He comes again at the end of the world.

prayer: Talking to God. You can use prayers you have learned or just tell Him what you are thinking.

priest: A man who has received the power from Jesus to forgive sins and offer Mass.

promise: To promise is to say you are going to do something and really mean it. God promised to send us a Savior.

prophets: Holy persons who prepared the people for the coming of Jesus, the Savior.

Queen of Heaven: The name we give to our Mother Mary to show that she has the highest place in Heaven next to Jesus. She is above all the angels and other saints.

Resurrection: The raising of a body from the dead. Jesus rose from the dead on Easter Sunday. Our bodies will be raised from the dead at the end of the world.

sacrifice: Showing God that we love Him the most by giving up something that we like.

saint: A holy person who loved God very much on earth and who is now in Heaven. God wants us all to be saints.

Savior: The one God promised to send to save us from our sins. Jesus is the Savior.

serve: To serve is to follow orders or to help or do work for someone else. We serve God when we do what He wants us to do.

shepherds: Men who take care of sheep. When Jesus was born some shepherds were the first to hear the Good News.

Sign of the Cross: The shape of a cross that we make by touching the forehead, chest, and shoulders to show that we believe that Jesus died on the Cross for us. We also show that we believe in the Blessed Trinity.

sin: Any bad thing that we do, think, or say. When we sin, we turn away from God.

soul: The part of us that thinks, loves, and chooses what to do. The soul never dies.

teacher: Someone who shares with others things that he knows so that they can know them, too.

Ten Commandments: Laws that God gave to Moses.

Trinity: The three divine Persons in one God. The Trinity is a mystery.

wise men: Men who knew many things about God and the world He made. Three wise men came to Jesus when He was a baby and brought Him presents fit for a king.

worship: To worship is to give your best love and praise to God.

The Alphabet

A is for *Apostles*, the twelve friends of Jesus.

A is also for *angels*, *Abraham*, *Adam*, *Alleluia*, *ark*, and *Ascension*.

B is for *Baptism*, the first sacrament. Baptism washes away sins and makes us God's children.

B is also for *Bethlehem*, *Bible*, *bishop*, *body*, and *believe*.

C is for *Catholic Church*, God's family.

C is also for *Cross*, *Christmas*, *Creator*, *Creed*, and *carpenter*.

D is for *devil*, an angel who turned away from God and who wants us to sin.

E is for *Easter*, the day Jesus rose from the dead.

F is for *forgive*. Jesus washes away sin.

G is for *God*, *our Father*, Who made everything and loves us all.

G is also for *Gabriel*, *Good Friday*, *Good News*, *Gospel*, *grace*, *genuflect*, and *guardian angel*.

H is for *Heaven*, where we will be happy with God for ever.

H is for *Holy Communion* and *Holy Spirit*.

I is for *Israel*, the land where Jesus was born.

J is for *Jesus*, the Son of God. He is our Savior and brother.

J is also for *John the Baptist* and *Joseph*.

K is for *king*. Jesus is the King of Heaven and earth.

L is for *Last Supper*, the dinner that Jesus ate with His Apostles the night before He died.

M is for *Mary*, the Mother of God and our Blessed Mother, too.

M is also for *Mass*, *Moses*, *manger*, *miracle*, and *mystery*.

N is for *Noah*. He obeyed God and saved his family and the animals from the flood.

N is also for *Nazareth*.

O is for *obey*. We must obey God's laws. God also wants us to obey our parents.

O is also for *Our Father* and *original sin*.

P is for *Pope*, the leader of the whole Church. He has the power to teach all Christians.

P is also for *prayer*, *Peter*, *priest*, *promise*, and *prophet*.

Q is for *quiet*. We are quiet in Church so we can pray and hear God's word.

Q is also for *Queen of Heaven*.

R is for *Resurrection*, the moment when Jesus was raised to new life.

S is for *saint*, someone who loved God on earth and is now in Heaven. There is a saint for almost every name. We all want to be saints, too.

S is also for *Savior*, *sin*, *sacrifice*, *serve*, *shepherd*, *Sign of the Cross*, and *soul*.

T is for *Trinity*, Three Persons in One God: the Father, Son, and Holy Spirit.

T is also for *Ten Commandments* and *teacher*.

U is for *unity*. All Catholics share the same faith in Jesus. We hope that everyone will share our faith someday.

V is for *victory*. Jesus won back the life of grace for us. He conquered sin and death.

W is for *wise men*. Three wise men came to adore the Child Jesus and bring Him presents.

W is also for *worship*.

X is for *Xmas*, which is another name for Christmas. The X stands for Christ, a name for Jesus.

Y is for *You*, a member of God's family. You can know, love, and serve God. You can be a saint!

Z is for *zeal*, another name for our love of God.

We Pray

THE SIGN OF THE CROSS

In the Name of the Father, and of the Son, and of the Holy Spirit. *Amen*.

GLORY BE

Glory be to the Father, and to the Son, and to the Holy Spirit, as it was in the beginning, is now, and ever shall be, world without end. *Amen*.

HAIL MARY

Hail Mary, full of grace! The Lord is with thee. Blessed art thou among women, and blessed is the fruit of thy womb, Jesus.
Holy Mary, Mother of God, pray for us sinners, now and at the hour of our death. *Amen*.

OUR FATHER

Our Father, Who art in Heaven, hallowed be
Thy Name; Thy Kingdom come; Thy will be
done on earth as it is in Heaven. Give us this day
our daily bread, and forgive us our trespasses as
we forgive those who trespass against us; and
lead us not into temptation, but deliver us from
evil. *Amen*.

PRAYER TO MY GUARDIAN ANGEL

Angel of God, my guardian dear,
To whom God's love commits me here,
Ever this day be at my side,
To light and guard, to rule and guide. *Amen*.

Art Credits